Mastering You

G000099222

2019 Updated iPad Pro User Guide and the New iPadOS 13 for Beginners and New iPad Users

Tech Reviewer

TABLE OF CONTENT

4

How to Use this Book

Welcome! Thank you for purchasing this book and trusting us to lead you right in operating your iPad Pro device. This book has covered every details and tips you need to know about the upgrading and operating your iPad Pro on the new iOS 13 and iPadOS for to ensure you get the best from your smart device.

To better understand how the book is structured, I would advise you read from page to page after which you can then navigate to particular sections as well as make reference to a topic individually. This book has been written in the simplest form to ensure that every user understands and gets the best out of this book. The table of content is also well outlined to make it easy for you to reference topics as needed at the speed of light.

Thank you.

Introduction

The 2018 iPad Pro with its 11-inch and 12.9-inch screen display comes with lots of exciting features like editing video, playing 3D games, drawing, writing, watching videos, reading and listening to music. You can also perform two or more functions simultaneously like you would on a desktop computer or laptop. The iPad Pro gives you that real computer experience. The smart device has slimmer bezels, a boxier design, and Face ID feature, which is quite awesome. The several features of the iPad Pro make it more powerful than other competing tablets and even any iOS devices launched before it, and with the right apps, you can perform wonders on your iPad Pro.

However, users of the iPad Pro had complained of several cons to using the smart device like the absence of headphone jack and the fact that you would need to purchase the accessories like the Apple Pencil 2 and the smart keyboard separately. The iPad Pro is the only iPad that supports the Apple Pencil 2, however, the pencil is not included in the cost of the iPad, you would need to purchase the pencil separately if you want to enjoy the features that comes with the Apple Pencil.

The iPad Pro was launched on the iOS 12 software which limited the amount of multitasking you can do on the iPad. The good news is that there is a new iOS 13 upgrade as well as an iPadOS software specially designed for iPads to improve the multitasking feature of your device along with several other functions.

To start with, the iPadOS has almost all the features that you would find in the iOS 13 like the revamped photo app, updated Maps, a new Dark Mode, performance optimization, Sign In with Apple, Find My app and several other features that will be discussed in this book. You would find all the features from the iPadOS and the iOS 13 that applies to the iPad device in this book to give you an optimal performance of your device.

Features of iPadOS

- Better Multitasking
- Support for external drive
- Introduction of Dark Mode
- Availability of expanded markups
- Reduced Apple Pencil latency
- Improvement on text editing

- Download manager now available in Safari
- New keyboard shortcuts

Updates to Multitasking

We have always been able to open multiple windows on the iOS device as well as the iPad. However, Apple has added some improvements that would make the multitasking more functional and powerful. The **Slide Over Multitasking** and **Split View** option now supports using multiple windows in a single app, this means that you can open more than one Safari browser alongside each other. When you launch the Slide Over view, you would see the new option to switch and view multiple apps with the interface of the **Slide Over card.**

This function makes it easy to open the same app in multiple places so that you can have multiple windows open at the same time while you use the App switcher to swap between the various open apps. To create windows, simply drag contents from one window into its own designed space. For example, drag a location to launch Maps, a link to Launch Safari as well as an email address to launch Mail.

New Home Screen

When Apple separated the iOS 13 and iPadOS, it made it possible for them to create a bigger screen for the iPad. One of such changes is the Home screen redesign specific to the iPad for a bigger screen display. The iPadOS now has a new home screen for the iPad device which reduces the size of the app icons to give room for more apps on each page. Icons located in the home screen are now smaller and so, you have enough space to fit in more icons on each of the home screen along with the new handy widget feature.

There is also the **Today Widgets** which you can add from the left side of your screen to your home screen to give you an easy access to your widgets as well as quick view of information like weather, news headlines, events and other important information when you set your device to landscape mode. Whenever you are in portrait mode, simply swipe to the right on your home screen to access your widgets. To customize the widgets on the home screen, click on **Edit** at the bottom of your screen. You would only see all your favorite widgets on the Home screen but to see all the other widgets, simply swipe to the right to access the **Today View Widgets.**

Files App

With the iPadOS Files app, you can now share folders from the iCloud Drive, this means you can send whole file folders to other people and there is also support for using external drive, which is the first time for witnessing this feature in iPad. You can plug in an SD card or USB drive and move data from the drive to the Files app, a feature that has been available on the iPhone before now. You can now make use of SD cards, SSDs, USB drives, SMB file servers, and others to access files you need from inside the Files app. You can also store files directly on your iPad local storage rather than on the iCloud storage.

There is also a new **"Column View" located in the Files app** that allows you to view high resolution previews of your files when your device is in landscape mode. **Support for Quick Actions** allows you to perform things like rotate images, mark up and create PDFs.

IPadOS also comes with support for zip and unzip, local storage and **30 new keyboard shortcuts.**

Slide Over
The slide over interface gives you the option to view and quickly switch between several apps. So, you can open multiple apps and then flip between them as you need, similar to opening several windows on a Mac. The Slide Over feature has made it easy for you to access things like Calendar or Messages quickly while browsing the web or working on a document with the Split View interface.

You can store all the apps you need to occasionally access in the **Slide Over** card and then tap to swap between them. To see all your apps in the Slide Over, simply swipe up and to get an app on Slide Over to go full screen, drag the app upwards. To close an app window in the Slide Over, go to App Switcher and then flick upwards on the app you wish to close.

Support for S controllers and PlayStation DualShock 4
Another new feature of the iPadOS is the controller support Xbox One S controllers and PlayStation

DualShock 4 and this means you do not need a Made for iPhone controller any longer to play games on your iPad. You can connect these new controllers via the Bluetooth.

APP EXPOSÉ
Another new feature is the App Exposé which displays when you hold down on the icon of an app. This feature allows you to view all the open windows of a specific app and you also have the option to swap between the open windows by a simple tap. With this feature, you can easily see all the apps that you have open as well as swap between tasks.

Improvements to the Apple Pencil
The iPadOS has made the Apple Pencil to be more deeply integrated to the iPad by using the Markup tool that is available in the operating system. Apple also included a reduced latency of the Apple pencil from **20** milliseconds **to 9** milliseconds.

Markup

When you use the Apple Pencil to tap on the corner of the iPad's display, it would open up Markup, which you can use for anything from documents and webpages to screenshots and emails. You can edit and annotate entire documents, webpages or emails using the Markup Feature with a simple swipe of the Apple Pencil from the corner of your screen. To take a screenshot, drag the Apple pencil from the bottom side of your iPad device.

Apple also has a restructured tool palette that you can use to quickly access tools that you use frequently along with shapes, color palettes, object eraser and a new pixel eraser to remove any part of a stroke. There is also the new ruler used for drawing straight lines. You can move the tool palette anywhere on your device screen to allow you customize the way you work. You would find this new tool palette in the Markup and the feature was also made available to 3rd party developers as an API.

Text Editing
Similar to the iPhone, it is now better to edit text on iPad thanks to the swipe gesture that was newly introduced as it allows you to select text as well as make use of the new gestures to copy, cut, undo and paste. You can use

the scroll bar to scroll through long web pages and documents by moving it upwards or downwards which is faster than just swiping. You can also drag your fingers over a text to select the text.

Double tap on a word to select it, triple tap to select an entire sentence or quadruple tap to select a complete paragraph. Double tapping makes it easy and fast to select elements like email addresses, phone numbers, and addresses. You can move the cursor to a desired location by simply clicking and dragging the cursor, this is faster than the previous software. Use your three fingers to pinch up on a word to copy the word, use your fingers to pinch up twice to cut and pinch down using the 3 fingers to paste. To redo and undo, use your 3 fingers to swipe to the right and to the left. To select multiple folders, files or email messages, simply tap with two fingers and then use the drag gesture.

You can now install fonts on your device along with a floating keyboard that allows you to type single handed due to the new QuickPath swipe feature. To enable the new floating keyboard, pinch in on the keyboard and drag it to your desired location on your device screen.

Safari

With this new iPadOS 13 software, whenever you launch Safari on your iPad, it would automatically take you to the desktop version of the website rather the mobile version. Now, you no longer have to force your browser to display the desktop version. Websites are now appropriately scaled to match the iPad's display as well as optimized for touch which means that you can make use of your favorite web apps like Slack, WordPress, Google Docs and Squarespace to do just about everything you could do on your Mac.

For the first time, Apple has included a download manager to the Safari browser which has made it easy to manage files downloaded from the web on the iPad, there are also improvements to how you manage open tabs. When you use Safari in the Split View, you would see the full Safari toolbar displayed.

Mouse Support

For the first time, you can make use of a mouse to operate your iPad by connecting it to the iPad. This feature is not enabled automatically as you would have to activate the **AssistiveTouch** option in the settings app which I would explain in details at a later part of this guide.

Long Press Gestures

You can also perform long press gestures on your iPad for things like link previews, Quick Actions and lots more, all thanks to the Haptic Touch that is available on the iPhone 11 models and the XR. Apple replaced the 3D Touch with the Haptic Touch to be able to achieve this feat. Long press on an app to display the Quick Actions like peeking into a link to see a little preview of the link. Although you would not get a haptic feedback response as you may see on the iPhone, but be rest assured that the feature is available on the iPad.

Sidecar

Once the macOS Catalina becomes available, your iPad can serve as a secondary display for your Mac device either by mirroring your Mac or by extending the display of your Mac device to your iPad. This feature allows you to use apps like Illustrator or Photoshop right on your iPad and they can successfully work with the Apple Pencil. Apart from drawing, you can use the Apple Pencil to point and click in same way you use a mouse. You can create a sketch on your iPad and then insert it on any document stored on Mac or sketch and write on PDFs for documents and view the updates directly on Mac. You can use the Sidecar with a cable or wireless connection within 10 meters and you have to set it up from a Mac for it to work.

Getting Started: How to Set up the iPad

You can set up the iPad over internet connection or by connecting it to your computer. You can transfer data to your new iPad from your iPad, iPhone, iPod touch or even an Android device.

Note: if a school, company or organization manages or deployed the iPad for you, you would need to meet with the teacher or administrator for setup instructions.

Items You Need for Set up

To ensure that you have a smooth setup, ensure to have the items below available

- Internet connection either via a cellular data service or via a Wi-Fi network. You would need the name and password if the network is protected.
- An Apple ID user name and password, if you do not have one already, you can create during the setup process.
- Your debit or credit card details if you would like to complete the Apple Pay process during set up.
- A backup of your device (if you intend to transfer data to your new device) or your old iPad.

- An android device if transferring content via android.

Steps to Setup your Device

- Press and hold down the button at the top until you see the Apple logo on your screen.
- You would see the "Hello" greeting appear on your screen in multiple languages. You can activate the **Voice Over or Zoom Option on this screen,** which is helpful for the blind or those with low vision.

- Select your language, then click on your country and region. Ensure to select the right information as it would affect how information like time, date and more would appear on your device.

- You can also click on tap the blue accessibility button to set up your accessibility options for optimizing your setup experience.
- If you want to set up the device manually, click on **Set Up Manually** then follow the instructions on your screen to set up your device.
- If you have an iPad, iPhone or an iPod touch operating on iPadOS 13, iOS 11 or later, you can click on **Quick Start** to set up your device automatically.
- Place the two devices beside each other then follow the instructions on your screen to securely copy several preferences, settings and iCloud Keychain from the other device to your new iPad.
- You can restore the remaining contents and data from the iCloud backup.
- Or, if both devices are on iPadOS 13 or iOS 12.4 or later, you can wirelessly transfer all your data from the previous device to your new iPad.
- Place both devices beside each other.
- Let both devices remain plugged into power until the transfer process is finished.

- If you have low vision or blind, click on the Home button three times to activate **VoiceOver**, the screen reader.

- Another way to transfer your data is by using a wired connection. You would see below steps to do this.

- Now, you have to connect your device to a cellular or Wi-Fi network or iTunes to activate your phone and continue with the setup. You should have inserted the SIM card before turning on the iPad if going with the cellular network option. To connect to a Wi-Fi network, just tap the name of your Wi-fi and it connects automatically if there is no password on the Wi-fi. If there is a security lock on the Wi-fi, the screen would prompt you for the password before it connects.

- Next is to set up your Face ID. The face ID feature gives you access to authorize purchases and unlock your devices. To setup the Face ID now, tap **Continue** and follow the instructions on the screen. You can push this to a later time by selecting **"Set Up Later in Settings**."

- Whether you setup Face ID now or later, you would be required to create a four-digit passcode to safeguard your data. This passcode is needed to access Face ID and Apple Pay. Tap **"Passcode Option"** if you would rather set up a four-digit passcode, custom passcode or even no passcode.

- If you have an existing iTunes or iCloud backup, or even an Android device, you can restore the backed-up data to your new phone or move data from the old phone to the new iPhone. To restore using iCloud, choose **"Restore from iCloud Backup"** or **"Restore from iTunes Backup"** to restore from iTunes to your new iPad. In the absence of any backup or if this is your first device then select **"Set Up as New iPad".**

- To continue, you would need to enter your Apple ID. If you have an existing Apple account, just enter the ID and password to sign in. In case you don't have an existing Apple ID or may have forgotten the login details, then select **Don't have an Apple ID or forget it.** If you belong to the class that have multiple Apple ID, then select **Use different Apple IDs for iCloud & iTunes** on the screen of the device.

- To proceed, you need to accept the iOS terms and conditions.
- Next is to set up Siri and other services needed on your device. Siri needs to learn your voice so you would need to speak few words to Siri at this point. You can also set up the iCloud keychain and Apple Pay at this point.

- Set up screen time. This would let you know the amount of time you spend on your device. You can also set time limits for your daily app usage.
- Now turn on automatic update and other important features.
- Click on **"Get Started"** to complete the process. And now, you can explore and enjoy your device.

Note: if the iPad doesn't come on, it may need to be charged.

How to Move Contents from an Android Device to the iPad

When setting up your new iPad, you can securely and automatically move data to your iPad from an android device. Please note that the **Move to iOS** app only works when you are setting up the iPad for the first time. To use this feature after you have completed setup, you would need to erase the iPad and begin afresh or just manually move your data.

When you first set up your new iPad, you can automatically and securely move your data from an Android device.

- Connect to Wi-Fi on your Android device.

- Ensure that the android device and the new iPad are plugged into power.

- Confirm that your new device has enough space to contain the items you want to move. To transfer your Chrome bookmarks, you have to be on the latest Chrome version on your Android device.

- Download the **Move to iOS** app to your android device.

- Go to your iPad, follow the set-up assistant, click on **Apps & Data screen.**

- Then click on **Move Data from Android.**

- Go to your android device and launch the **Move to iOS** app.

- Click on **Continue** in the app.

- Terms and conditions would appear on the next screen. Read and then click on **Agree.**

- Click on **Next** in the screen for **Find Your Code** in the android device.

- Go to your iPad device and click on **Continue** in the screen for **Move from Android.**

- You would receive a 6- or 10-digit code on your iPad screen. If you receive an alert of weak connection from your Android, ignore the alert.

- Input the displayed code into the Android device, then you would see the screen for **Transfer Data.**

- Select the contents you want to move from your Android device then click on **Next.**

- Even if you receive a notification on your android that the process is complete, it is best to allow both devices be until you can see that the loading bar in your iPad loads completely. It can take some time to complete the transfer, usually dependent on how large the contents you are moving.

- The contents that you can transfer include: messages, contacts, camera videos and photos, history, web bookmarks, calendars and mail accounts. When the transfer is completed, you can redownload all the free apps matched from the app store.

- Once the loading bar is completed on your iPad, go to your android device and click on **Done.**

- Then click on **Continue** on your iPad and follow the steps in the setup guide above to complete the setup process.

How to Transfer Data Using Quick Start Option from the Previous iOS to your iPad

You can move contents and data from your previous iPod, iPad or iPad to your most recent device. Quick Start allows you to quickly set up your new device from data from the previous one. When using Quick Start you may be unable to do any other thing on both devices, so it is important you perform this process when you would not need to make use of your devices for some minutes.

- Power on your iPad and position it close to your previous device.

- The **Quick Start** screen would appear on the screen of your current device while setting up the new iPad with the option to set up your new iPad using Apple ID.

- Confirm the Apple ID is the right one before you click on **Continue.**

- If you cannot find the option for **Continue** on your old device, ensure your Bluetooth is activated.

- Allow some seconds for an animation to show on your new device.

- Hold your old device over the new iPad and position the animation to fit into the viewfinder.

- You would receive a message on the screen reading, **Finish on New [Device].**

- If you do not want to make use of the camera in your current device, click on **Authenticate Manually** and follow the instructions you would see on your screen.

- When asked, input the passcode for the current device into the new iPad.

- Follow the instructions on your new iPad to set up Face ID or Touch ID.

- Input the Apple ID on your iPad when prompted.

- Your new iPad would give you options of restoring data, apps and settings from the last iCloud backup or to first, update backup on your current device before restoring on the new one. Choose a backup and then select whether you wan to transfer some settings related to privacy, location, Siri and Apple Pay.

- Ensure that you are connected to a strong Wi-Fi network before you update backup on your device.

How to Restart Your iPad

- Press and hold down the button at the top of your device along with any of the volume button until you see the power off slider on your screen
- Drag the slider to the right to turn off your device.
- Press and hold down on the top button again to power on the device. Hold down until you see the Apple logo.

How to Download iPadOS/ iOS 13 on iPad
To be able to enjoy the features packed in the iPadOS/ iOS 13, you first have to download it on your iPad. First step is to ensure that your iPad has been backed up to

make it easy for you to restore your device in case you lose your contents during the upgrade.

How to Backup Using iCloud
This is probably the simplest way to back up your device with the steps below

- Connect your device to a Wi-Fi network.
- Go to the settings app.

- Click on your name at the top of the screen.
- Then click on **iCloud**.
- Navigate down and click on **iCloud backup**.
- Then select **Back Up Now.**

To check whether the backup was completed, follow the steps below

- Go to settings.
- Click on **iCloud.**
- Then select **iCloud BackUp.**
- Navigate to **iCloud Backup,** there you would see the time and date of your last backup.

How to Back Up on MacOS Catalina
Although the MacOS 10.15 Catalina no longer has the iTunes icon as they replaced it with apps for Podcasts, Books and Music, you can still use the new MacOS to back up your iPhone device.

- Connect your iPad device to the Mac and ensure its updated.
- Follow the instructions on the screen and enter your passcode if requested or activate the *Trust This Computer* option.
- Launch the **Finder App.**
- Choose your iPad device from the side bar.
- Click on **General.**

- Then click on **Back Up Now** *to begin a manual backup.*

How to Back Up with iTunes on PC or Mac
if you have a Windows PC or an older Mac, you can use the iTunes to back up your iPad with the steps below:

- Confirm that the iTunes is updated to the current version then launch iTunes and connect your iPad to the PC.
- Follow the instructions on the screen and enter your passcode if requested or activate the **Trust This Computer** option.
- In the iTunes app, click on your iPad.
- Then click on **Back Up Now** to back up your device.
- To confirm that the backup was successful, navigate to **Latest Backup** to see the date and time of the last backup.

How to Download and Install iPadOS/ iOS 13 on your iPad
The best way to download iOS 13 on your iPad is via the air with the steps below

- Go to the settings app

- Click on **General**

- Then select **Software Update**

- Your device would begin to search for a new update after which you would receive notification of the iOS 13.1.

- Click on **Download and Install.**

- It may take a while to download and you would not be able to make use of your device during the update.

How to Download and Install iPadOS/ iOS 13 on PC or Mac Through iTunes

If you would rather download the iOS 13 to your PC or Mac through iTunes, use the highlighted steps below:

- You have to be on the most current version of iTunes.
- Connect the iPad to your computer.
- Launch iTunes then click on your iPad.
- On the next screen, select **Summary.**
- Then click on **Check for Update.**
- *Finally click on* **Download and Update.**

How to Hard Reset your iPad Device

Most challenges you encounter with your device can be resolved by restarting your iPad. However, the normal restart process may not always work. There are times you may not even see the slider and the iPad would refuse to respond to touch, in cases like these, a hard reset is needed. This step would not clear data from your phone but would only delete the memory for the operating system and apps. The steps below would show you how to perform a hard reset.

- Press and hold both the top button and the home button at same time.
- Continue to hold the buttons until the screen goes black. Ignore the slider at this stage.
- Release the buttons only when the Apple logo shows on your screen.
- The device would start up normally.

How to Erase Your iPad Settings and Data

You can choose to delete some specific settings from your device or restore the iPad back to default factory settings.

A factory reset would erase every data stored on your iPad and return the device back to its original form from the stores. Every single data from settings to personal data saved on the phone will be deleted. It is important you create a backup before you go through this process. You can either backup to iCloud or to iTunes. Once you have successfully backed up your data, please follow the steps below to wipe your phone.

- From the **Home** screen, click on **Settings.**
- Click on **General.**
- Select **Reset.**

- Chose the option that suits what your need.

- For factory reset, select **Erase All Content and Settings**. This would return the phone to its status from the store.

- Click on **Reset All Settings** if you want to reset just your settings without erasing your apps and data.

- When you click on **Reset Network Settings,** it would restore your wireless network settings to factory default.

- **Reset Keyboard Dictionary** option would delete all the spellings and words you added to your device's spellchecker/ dictionary.

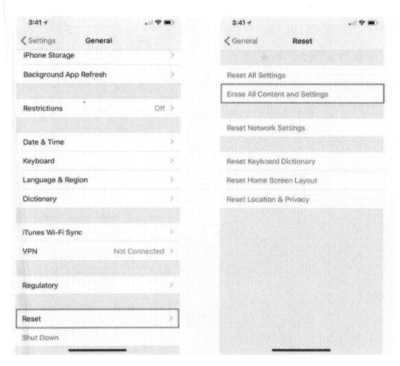

- **Reset Home Screen Layout** option would disable all the arrangements of apps and folders you have and return the home screen layout to default.

- **Reset Location and Privacy** option would delete all the permissions on your device and then the apps would have to request for the permissions afresh.

- When asked, enter your passcode to proceed.

- Click **Erase iPhone** to approve the action.

Depending on the volume of data on your phone, it may take some time for the factory reset to be completed.

Once the reset is done, you may choose to setup with the **iOS Setup Assistant/Wizard** where you can choose to restore data from a previous iOS or proceed to set the device as a fresh one.

How to Backup Using iCloud

This is probably the simplest way to back up your device with the steps below

- Connect your device to a Wi-Fi network.
- Go to the settings app.

- Click on your name at the top of the screen.
- Then click on **iCloud**.
- Navigate down and click on **iCloud backup**.
- Then select **Back Up Now.**

To check whether the backup was completed, follow the steps below

- Go to settings.
- Click on **iCloud.**
- Then select **iCloud BackUp.**
- Navigate to **iCloud Backup,** there you would see the time and date of your last backup.

How to Back Up on MacOS Catalina

Although the MacOS 10.15 Catalina no longer has the iTunes icon as they replaced it with apps for Podcasts, Books and Music, you can still use the new MacOS to back up your iPhone device.

- Connect your iPad device to the Mac and ensure its updated.
- Follow the instructions on the screen and enter your passcode if requested or activate the *Trust This Computer* option.

- Launch the **Finder App.**
- Choose your iPad device from the side bar.
- Click on **General.**
- Then click on *Back Up Now to begin a manual backup.*

How to Back Up with iTunes on PC or Mac

if you have a Windows PC or an older Mac, you can use the iTunes to back up your iPad with the steps below:

- Confirm that the iTunes is updated to the current version then launch iTunes and connect your iPad to the PC.
- Follow the instructions on the screen and enter your passcode if requested or activate the **Trust This Computer** option.
- In the iTunes app, click on your iPad.
- Then click on **Back Up Now** to back up your device.
- To confirm that the backup was successful, navigate to **Latest Backup** to see the date and time of the last backup.

How to Use Cycle Tracking in Health

The health app in the Apple device is a great tool and the iOS 13 has brought more additions, the biggest of this addition is the cycle tracking. With this tool, you can track your menstrual cycle and also have tools to alert you when you are at your most fertile days and when you are due. To get started, follow the steps below

- Launch the health app.
- Then choose **Search**, and click on **Cycle tracking** from the displayed list.
- Click on **Get started**, then click on **Next.**
- The app would ask you series of questions like duration of your period and the date the last one started.
- You would also get options on ways you would like to track your period; you can also choose to be given notifications and predictions on when you are likely to see the next cycle. You would also select whether you would like to record spotting and symptoms in your cycle log and whether you want to be able to view your fertility Windows.

- As soon as you have provided all the answers, you would return to the homepage for **Cycle Tracking.**
- On this screen, click om **Add Period** to choose days that you have experienced your periods.
- You can also click on Spotting, **Symptoms** and Flow Levels option to input more specific details.

How to Use the Find My App

In the iOS 13, Apple combined the Find My iPhone and Find My Friends feature into an app they called **Find My.** With this feature you can share your location to your loved ones and friends as well as find your devices using the same app. It is simple to use with the steps below

- Go to your home page and launch the **Find My** app.
- Under the **People** tab, you would sew your current location.
- Click on the **Start Sharing Location** tab to share with a contact.
- Type in your desired contact to share with.

To find your missing device,

- Click on the **Device** tab to modify your map to present all the registered Apple devices on your account.
- Click on the missing device then select from any of the options on the screen: ***Mark As Lost*, Get Directions** to the device, **remotely *Erase This Device*, or *Play Sound.***
- *If any of the device is currently offline, you can set the map to alert you once the device is connected to the internet. Simply click the **Notify Me** option.*

How to Edit Photos and Rotate Videos

Other iOS had lacked its own editing tools until the iOS 13. Now, you can go to your photo app to modify various key parts of your videos and photos. The improved and new photo editor located in the Photos app is the perfect replacement for Darkroom or Snapseed when it comes to basic editing of images. It has the same Instagram editing style interface in a simpler way. It also includes more features for editing like brilliance, vibrance and more. Follow the steps below to edit your photos and videos.

- Go to your photos app.
- Choose your desired photo and then click on the **Edit** button.
- On the next screen, you can try to swipe between options and adjust sliders to see how your picture would look when modified with several options
- You can also do this for the videos.

How to Use Sign-IN-With-Apple

It can be quite tiring having to log in each time you launch a different app and at the same time you may not be comfortable signing in with your Instagram account to all apps. The Sign in with Apple allows you to quickly sign into apps with your Apple account while protecting the need to not share personal information.

- For apps that support this feature, you would see the option displayed on the opening screen of the apps.

- Click on it and you would be prompted to login to your Apple account
- Then you would select the information you desire to share with the app developer.
- With this feature, you can decide to share your email address or not to share it.
- If you do not want to share your personal email address, Apple would generate a random email address that would automatically forward to your Apple iCloud email address while keeping your anonymity safe.

How to Use the Apple Pencil with your iPad

The Apple pencil gives you opportunities to perform several functions on your iPad from putting your signature to a document to sketching and drawing. Thankfully, the iPad Pro support the 2nd generation Apple Pencil.

How to Create a New Note with Apple Pencil on Lock Screen

If you are looking for a quick way to create a new note, follow the steps below:

- First is to wake your device.
- Then use the Apple pencil to click on your screen.
- A new note would appear on your screen instantly.
- To reposition the markup toolbar, simply drag it to any edge.

How to Create a Signature with the Apple Pencil

- From the bottom corner of your device screen, swipe all the way up.
- Click on the Plus (+) sign in the Markup Toolbar.
- Select **Signature.**
- On the popup field, sign your name.
- Click on **Done** after you have inputted your signature.
- the next time you need to input your signature, you would not have to sign it again.
- Simply click on the Plus (+) sign in the Markup toolbar of every app that supports this feature.
- Then click on **Signature.**

How to Sketch and Draw with the Apple Pencil

This is quite easy. The Apple Pencil allows you to markup, draw and write with apps from the App store as well as in built apps. Some apps like Notes allow you to sketch and draw with the Apple Pencil.

The iPadOS comes with a redesigned tool palette. Move the palette around the screen or minimize it if you want more space to sketch and draw.

Use the ruler tool to make straight lines, then use your fingers to rotate them. If you made any mistakes, you can either erase by pixel or by object. To write and draw with your Apple pencil, position your palm on the screen display without it registering like a mark. Increase your hand pressure when drawing thicker lines, to shade, tilt your pencil.

How to Pair Your Apple Pencil with Your iPad (2nd generation)

- Fix the apple pencil into the magnetic connector on the side of your iPad Pro as shown in the image below:

How to Unpair Your Apple Pencil with Your iPad

Whenever your Apple pencil is paired with your device it would remain paired until you turn on Airplane Mode, restart your device or pair the Apple pencil to another iPad device.

How to Sketch or Draw in the Notes App

- Open the Note app.
- Click on ⬜ to begin a new note.
- Click on Ⓐ to draw. If you do not find the symbol, you would need to update your Notes app. Click on Ⓐ to sketch.
- Then begin to sketch or draw.
- Select from the different colors and drawing tools.
- Whenever you make a mistake, switch to eraser to clean it.
- Double click on the eraser to see the options for erasing on your device.
- Press your pencil firmly on your screen to darken a line or tilt to shade a line.

Note: you can now draw on any part of your screen without activating the Notification Center, Control Center or Multitasking mistakenly.

Double Clicking your Apple Pencil (Second Generation)

With your second-generation Apple pencil, double click on the lower part of the pencil for a fast switch back to the tool that you used last. If you wish to change what happens when you double click the lower part of the pencil, follow the steps below:

- Go to **Settings**
- Click on **Apple Pencil.**
- Then select between any of the 4 options below:

- "Show color palette"
- "Switch between current tool and last used"
- "Switch between current tool and eraser"
- "Off"

How to Charge Your Apple Pencil (Second Generation)
- Ensure that the Bluetooth is enabled on your iPad.
- Then fit in your pencil to the magnetic connector at the middle of your iPad close to the right side.

- To know how much time is left for the pencil to fully charge, go to the widgets view on your device.

Note: When using your iPad Pro to charge your Apple Pencil and your car's keyless entry device (key fob) is close by, the signal interference may not allow you to unlock the car with the key fob. When you encounter this, simply distance the key fop from the iPad Pro or even remove the pencil from the iPad and keep aside. Once the Pencil is fully charged, you would notice that all the signal interference would stop.

What to Do if Your Apple Pencil Refuse to Pair with the iPad

- Ensure that the Apple Pencil is well placed on the magnetic connector to the right side of the iPad.
- Restart your iPad device before you attempt to pair again.
- Check that Bluetooth is enabled. Go to **Settings** then click on **Bluetooth.**
- On that same screen, go to the section for **My Devices** and look for your Apple Pencil.
- When you locate your pencil, click on ⓘ.
- Then click on **Forget this Device.**
- Plug in the Apple Pencil to the iPad and then click on the **Pair** button after a few seconds.
- If the Pair button does not appear, allow some seconds for the Apple Pencil to charge. Then connect the pencil again and wait for the Pair button to show up.
- If the pair button still does not show up, then you would need to contact Apple Support.

How to Use the Apple Map

How to Use Favorites in the Apple Maps

I know that Apple map has been available for some time now but not so many like using it. Good news is that the IOS 13 has brought an improvement to the Apple map to include more beaches, roads, building and other details you may be interested in. Apart from these listed ones, there are also some other cool features that were just added like being able to add a location to your list of Favorites. You can also arrange the saved locations in your own personally customized collections. Follow the steps below to add a favorite on the map.

- Search for a location or tap on a location.
- Scroll down to the bottom and click on **Add to Favorites.**
- You can always access your favorites list on your main page.

To add a particular location to your customized collection,

- Drag up from the Apple maps main page.

- Then click on **My Places.**
- Select **Add a Place.**
- On the next screen, you can now add any location that you recently viewed to your collection or search through your search bar for the location.

To begin a new collection,

- Navigate back to your apple maps main page.
- Swipe from the bottom of the screen upwards.
- Then click on **New Collections** to make a new list.

How to Use the Look Around Feature in Apple Maps

Look around is Apple's version of the Streetview from Google as it allows you to preview a location before you visit. Follow the steps below on how to use it.

- Type in a location on your Apple maps.
- Then select it by pressing long on the map.
- If the location supports Look around you would find a **look around** image on the location.
- Click on it to move down to Street level and drag to navigate around.

- While on this view, you can also see facts about the place or even add it to your favorites list but swiping up from the bottom of the screen.

At the moment, Apple hasn't covered the whole locations in the USA but they have promised it do this by end of 2019 and also follow suite for other countries.

How to Mark Up Pages with the Apple Pencil

To take a screenshot of a page or to annotate it with the Apple pencil, simply use the Apple pencil to swipe in from the bottom side of your screen.

How to Search on your iPad

You can use the search button to find things quickly on your device and even on the web. When used with Siri, you would get suggestions and results while typing.

How to Swipe to Search

Need to quickly find an email, contact or restaurant nearby? You can do this from your Home screen

- From the middle of your home screen, swipe down.

- Click on the search filed and then begin to type your search keyword.

- As you are typing, search results would be updating real time.

- Click on **Show More** to see more results or you can go directly to the search in an app by clicking on **Search in App.**

- Click on a search result to launch it.

How to Change Search Settings

You can modify the search settings to limit the results and apps that appear whenever you search. Follow the steps below:

- Go to **Settings.**

- Click on **Siri & Search.**

- Navigate to your desired app and select it.

- Choose from either **Suggest Shortcuts, Show in Search,** or **Show Siri Suggestions** to prevent or allow shortcut suggestions and results from showing up.

- After turning off these features, you can also select the **Show App** feature.

- Disable this feature if you do not want the app to appear when you search.

- You can also turn on the "**Suggestions on Lock Screen"** to stop an app from showing up on the Lock screen under Siri suggestion.

How to Use Notifications on Your iPad

It is now easier to manage and view multiple notifications at the same time.

How to Access Notification from the Lock Screen

To view your notifications from the lock screen, follow the guide below:

- Wake up your iPad to quickly view your latest notifications.

- Click on a group of notifications or a single notification to view all the notification for that app.

- Swipe to the left of the notifications to view, manage or even clear off the notifications

- You can also manage alerts for specific apps on the lock screen.

How to Open Notification from Notification Center

You would find your notification history in the notification centre, allowing you to see what you may have missed. You can do this in two ways.

- While on the lock screen, swipe up from the center of the screen.

- While in any other screen, start swiping down from the middle of the display screen top.

- Click and hold the to clear the notification history, then click on **Clear All Notifications** or **Clear.**

How to Manage Notifications

- Swipe left on a group of alerts(s).

- Click on manage and then choose from the options below

- **Turn off** to disable all notifications for a particular app. To enable, go to **Settings** then click on **Notifications,** choose the app and then click on **Allow Notifications.**

- **Deliver Quietly** feature would show the notifications in the notification center alone without any sound or alert.

How to Change Alert Styles

To modify or add alert style for notification,

- Go to the settings app.

- Click on **Notification.**

- Under **Notification Style,** choose an app.

- Select your desired banner style and alert type.

- You can also enable or disable badges and sounds.

How to Change Group Notification Settings

You can either group your notifications or separate them.

- Go to the settings app.

- Click on **Notification.**

- Choose an app and click on **Notification Grouping.**

- Then select any of your preferred option.

How to Setup Location Based Alerts

Some apps alert you based on your location. For instance, you may receive a reminder to call someone when you get to a particular spot. You can turn off this setting with the steps below:

- Go to the settings app.

- Click on **Privacy.**

- Then click on **Location Services.**

- Click on individual apps to enable or disable.

How to Reduce Home Screen Icons Grid

The iPadOS 13 comes with the 5 by 6 grid by default. However, you can switch back to the old 5 by 5 grid with the steps below:

- Go to the settings app.
- Click on **Display and Brightness.**
- Navigate to the option for **App Icon Size** and then make your choice from any of the below:
- **More:** to get up to 30 apps displayed on your home screen by setting the app grid to 6 by 5 size.
- **Bigger:** to get up to 20 larger apps displayed on your home screen by fixing the apps at 4 by 5 grid.

How to Use your iPad as Second Mac Display

With the new Sidecar feature, you can now use your iPad for your Mac device that is operating the MacOS Catalina. You can use this whether with a wired connection or wirelessly. It has no latency and it is very fast. With an Apple pencil, you can use the attached iPad to serve as a drawing table for your Mac. Follow the steps below

- Connect your iPad device to your Mac PC either through wireless Bluetooth connection or using a charging cable.
- Ensure that both devices are on the same iCloud account.
- After the iPad is connected, go to your Mac and click on the menu for AirPlay.
- You would see your iPad listed on the menu.
- There are two available ways to set up the dual screen. You can either mirror the screens to have same display on both devices or extend your desktop display to the iPad to give two difference screens.
- If you want to extend your Mac PC to your iPad, click on this option. This option means that you can be doing one thing on your Mac and doing something different on the iPad like typing on the Mac while watching a video on the iPad.
- Select the option to **Mirror your two screens** if you want the same display on both the Mac and the iPad.

Note: this feature can be helpful when you want to carry out an activity on your iPad while you have people watching from the Mac. This means that several iPad features would be unavailable when you connect to Mac.

How to Use a Mouse with your iPad

With the new iPadOS, you can now connect a mouse to your iPad using the Accessibility feature. Follow the steps below to do this

- Go to the settings app.

- Navigate to **Accessibility.**

- Then enable **Assistive Touch.**

- Go to the section for **Devices** to set your iPad in pairing mode.

- Plug in your mouse to the iPad.

- A cursor would now show on your screen that you can move around.

- Right click on the mouse to launch the **Assistive Touch** menu while you left click to perform a finger tap.

- Go to the **Assistive Touch** menu to change the cursor size, tracking speed, cursor color and lots more.

How to Use Widgets on your iPad

Widget allows you to get quick information from your favorite applications at a glance.

How to Find Widgets in the Today View

- Go to the Home or Lock screen and swipe to the right to reveal the widgets in the Today View.
- if you wish to see more details from a widget, just click on **Show More.**
- To launch the app for the widget, simply click on the Widget.

How to Add or Remove Widgets from the Today View

Not only can you add and remove widgets, you can also rearrange them so that your favorite ones would stay at the top.

- Go to the Home or Lock screen and swipe to the right to reveal the widgets in the Today View.
- Navigate to the bottom of your screen and click on **Edit.**
- Click on ⊕ to add a widget, while you click on ⊖ to remove a widget.
- To rearrange your widgets, Tap and hold ☰ sign beside the apps and then pull them in your desired order.
- Then click on **Done.**

Note: you need to connect your iPad to another supported Bluetooth accessory or device to be able to view the Battery widget.

How to Use Quick Actions to Add and View Widgets

- Go to your home screen and then deep press an app icon to quickly see the information on stocks, weather and other information.
- Click on **Add Widget** to include the app to the Today View option.

How to Add Widgets to Home Screen

Not only can you now view your widgets on the home screen, you can also get them pinned to the home screen with the steps below:

- Go to the home screen and swipe to the right to display the widgets.
- To pin the widgets, navigate to the bottom of the **Today View** panel, then click on **Edit.**
- Go to **Keep on Home Screen** and move the switch to the right to activate this feature.

How to Work with Two Apps Simultaneously

Do you like chatting while browsing, you can now make use of the Split view to operate the two apps at once.

- Launch the first app.
- Then swipe from the bottom edge of your screen, pause to display the Dock.
- Then click and pull another app to the left or right side of your screen.
- To close the split view, drag the divider over an app.

How to Switch Quickly Between Your Favorite Apps

You can view apps in the Dock while using another app by swiping up from the bottom of the screen, then pause to see the Dock.

- Click on an app to launch it.
- Or click and pull another app over the Dock for the app to appear in a **Slide Over** window.
- To move to another app while using the **Slide Over** window, swipe from the end of the **Slide Over** window up and then click on an app.

How to Open Multiple Apps in Slide Over

Follow the steps below to open multiple apps in Slide Over.

- Launch the floating Slide Over panel
- Then activate the Dock.
- Pull an app icon over the open Slide Over window.
- You can move between the open windows by swiping right or left on the little home bar under the Slide Over panel.

How to Open Multiple Instances of a Single App

You can now open multiple windows of the same app either in a split screen or a new screen. For apps that support this feature, follow the step below:

- Click on a part of the app like the Mail or a Note.
- Pull it out of the app to the right edge of your screen.
- Once you get to the edge of the screen, release your finger to launch another window of that same app.
- To launch the window into full screen, move your finger to the top of the screen and release it.

How to See All Instances of the Same App Together

With the App Expose feature, you can now view all the open windows of a particular app in a single screen and then close the windows you no longer need. To do this,

- Open the desired app.
- Take up the dock and click on the app icon to see all the open Windows of a single app together.
- Swipe up on the window you wish to exit to close it.

How to Use External Storage with Files App

You can now connect external storage devices on your iPad to use in the Files app. This is great news for those that have the USB-C and have always desired to use the USB-C flash drives on their iPad devices. In fact, as long as you have the right cable, you can now use the Files app with a kindle. As long as you can get the external drive connected to the Files app, your device can read the storage.

- After it is connected, you would see it in the Sidebar of the Files app.

- Click on the Drive to access its directory.

- Click on the folders and files you wish to move and then drag them to your desired location whether it is the local storage or the iCloud Drive.

How to Customize Your Memoji and Animoji

Follow the steps below to design your own Memoji and Animoji.

- Go to iMessage.
- Tap on a conversation to launch it.
- Then click on the Memoji icon, then tap the "+" button.

How to Share Music Over AirPods

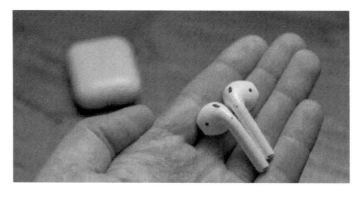

Now you can stream the same music across two Airpods pairs. To start, you have to pair your iPad with the second pair of Airpods. After that is done, you can now choose the second Airpods pair from the settings for Airplay in the same way you can choose your own.

- Connect the first AirPods to your iPad then position the second AirPod case beside the iPad.
- Then click on the **Round button** located at the back of the Airpods.
- Then click on **Connect**.
- After you have successfully paired the second device with your iPad, you would now see it as an option in the screen for Airplay.
- To select the second pair, click on the name.
- The audio would immediately go through the Airpods in sync.

How to Save Your Passwords

Similar to the iOS 12, you can have your logins and passwords saved to your iCloud keychain. Whenever you log in to a service, the system would prompt to ask if you would like to save your login details to the iCloud keychain. However, you can now manually manage your details. To do this,

- Go to **Settings.**
- Click on *Passwords & Accounts.*
- Then select *Website & App Passwords.*

- You may be prompted to use your passcode, Face ID or Touch ID to access this screen.

How to Set up Siri

To use Siri on your iPad, you have to set it up like you set up the Face ID. Find below the steps to do this.

- Click on **Siri & Search** from the **Settings** app.
- Beside the option **"Press Side Button for Siri"**, move the switch to the right to enable the function.
- A pop-up notification would appear on the screen, select **"Enable Siri"**.
- Switch on the **"Listen to Hey Siri"** option and follow the instructions you see on the screen of your iPhone. (To use Siri when your phone is locked, activate the **Allow Siri When Locked** option).
- Click on **language** and select the desired language.
- Click on the **< Siri & Search** button at the top left of the screen to go back.
- Scroll and select **Siri Voice.**
- On the next screen, select accent and gender.

- Click on the **< Siri & Search** button at the top left of the screen to go back.
- Select "**Voice Feedback**".
- Choose your preferred setting.
- Click on **< Siri & Search** at the top left of the screen.
- Select **My Information.**
- Click on the contact of choice. If you set yourself as the owner of the phone, the device would use your data for various voice control functions like navigating home. You can create yourself on the contact by following the steps given in creating contact.
- Select the desired application.
- Next to "**Search and Siri Suggestions**" slight left or right to turn on or off.

Now Siri is set up and ready to be used.

How to Activate Siri

There are 2 ways to activate Siri on your iPad.

- Voice option. If you enabled "Hey Siri", then you can begin by saying "Hey Siri" and then ask Siri any question.
- Using the side button. To wake Siri, press the side button and ask your questions. Once you release the side button, Siri stops listening.

How to Exit Siri

To exit Siri, follow the simple step below.

- Press the side button or swipe u from the bottom of the display to exit Siri.

How to Play Live Radio Through Siri

Although this feature was available in the iOS 12, however, the iOS 13 brought about some new additions. This function is quite easy. You can just say to Siri, "hey Siri, "play [name of radio station] radio station." As long as Siri have access to the requested radio station, it would begin to play it. Siri works with various online radio providers to be able to bring you your desired radio station.

How to Add Siri Shortcuts

This function lets you assign quick actions to your virtual assistant, Siri. While this feature came with the iOS 12, however, iOS 13 witnessed a more pronounced function for Siri and in the IOS 13, you have the Siri shortcut app on its own.

- To get started, click on the **shortcut app** to launch it

- Then click on **Create Shortcuts** to create a simple type of shortcut.

- With the **automation** tab, your device is able to intelligently react to context as they change, for instance you can customize the shortcut to play a particular song each time you get home or design the button to automatically send your location to your partner whenever you are heading home from work.

- In the **Gallery** function, you would find a range of predefined shortcuts to give you some inspiration in designing yours or you can even make use of the predefined shortcuts.

How to Use Screen Time

For those who have used iOS 12 before, you may be familiar with this feature. But in case you are not, it's quite simple to set up and it would help you to know how much time you are spending on your iPad. To begin with screen time,

- Go to **Settings**
- Then click on **Screen time.**

How to Set App Limits

If you really want to watch your usage, then you can set a duration on time spent in using a certain app with the App Limits feature available under Screen Time. The steps below would guide you on how to do it.

- Go to **Settings**
- Then click on **Screen time.**
- Select **App Limits.**
- Then click on **Add Limit.**

- Now the nee addition in iOS 13 allows you to choose apps that belong to a category and then group them together to have the same app limit. This means that you can limit your usage of Spotify, Twitter and Fortnite to a combined total of 6 hours every day.
- Once you hit the limit, you would get a splash screen notifying you that limit has been reached as well as give you the option to ignore the limit for the reminder of the day or just for 15 minutes only.

The New Reminders App

While the iOS 13 brought about entirely new features, it also modified the old ones with new additions. The default Apple reminders app was lacking in several features that you would find in other third-party to-do apps. Now the iOS 13 has modified the reminders app to include all the features that users would like. The steps below would guide you on how to use the new reminders app.

How to Use the New Reminders app

The iOS 13 brought a new built for the iOS reminders app. When you launch the reminders app, you can view the total reminders you have at the moment, the ones that are due today and the numbers that can be seen in each list. To add a new task to the list,

- Click on **All.**
- Then click the "+" button located underneath each category to add a new task

You can also add a reminder time or date, change the category for a task or set to be reminded of a task in a specified location by clicking on the 'I' icon in blue icon once you have tapped on the desired tasks to launch the options.

How to Create a Reminder

- First step is to launch the reminders app.
- Then click on **reminders** under **My List** heading
- Then select **New Reminders** at the bottom of your screen, at the left side.
- Fill in your details for the reminder.

- Then click **Return** on your keyboard to confirm your first reminder.

How to Add Location, Time or a Connected person

It's one time to add a reminder, it's another thing to have do go through your to-do to be reminded of what you intend to do in the day. Now you can add a time or location to your reminder so that your iPad can prod you at the right time or place. After you have set your reminder, click on the blue "i" icon that is located at the right side of your task to access the task options.

- To be reminded at a specific time, enable the option for *"Remind me on a day" and then fill in details in the option for "Alarm" or "Reminds me at a time".*
- *For recurring tasks, you can set the option to repeat.*
- *To add location, you should go for the option of Remind me at a location and then select your desired location*

- If your task has to do with someone, then you can set the reminder to alert you about the task whenever you message the contact. To do this, click on **Remind me when messaging** *and then choose your preferred contact.*

Get Siri to Remind You

With your virtual assistant, you do not always have to launch the reminders app and begin inputting details to remove an event or activity. You can say to Siri, "remind me to," followed by the contents of what you would like to be reminded on. You can also ask Siri to remind you at a specific place or time.

How to Add SubTasks

For complex projects or tasks, you can add sub tasks or you can even create a multi entry list for your shopping. If you have a reminder that needs to have the subtasks set,

- Go to the task from your reminder app.
- Click on the blue "i" icon to launch the options.

- Then navigate down on your screen to the option for **Subtasks**.
- Click on it and then tap **Add Reminder** to include a subtask.
- Feel free to add as many subtasks as you like.
- When you are done, you would find your subtask under the reminder or the main task.
- You can complete the subtasks separately from the parent task.
- You can also click on the "i" icon to add its own time, separate location or contacts for each individual subtask.

How to Use Today Notification Feature

You may have noticed that the reminders app has a new home page which is self-explanatory. However, there is one important feature that is not revealed. By default, the reminders app would notify you on the tasks you have for each day. But you can change when you want the notification to happen or if you want to be notified at all. To effect this change,

- Go to the settings app.
- Click on **Reminders.**
- On the next screen, you can completely turn off notifications or change the timing door the option of **Today Notification.**
- In this same screen, you can modify your tasks' default list.

How to Create a List

This new modifications in the reminder app can get us carried away with filling every little detail from tax notifications, to birthdays to grabbing milk on your way from work. The good thing is that you can organize your tasks into lists to declutter your reminders home page. The steps below would show you how to create a list.

- Launch the reminders app
- Then click on **Add list** found at the right bottom of the screen.
- Select from the varieties of logos and colors to help you tell the different lists at a glance.

- Once satisfied with your list, click on **Done** at the right top side of your screen.
- To add reminders or tasks to the list, click on the list from under the **My Lists** subheading and create them or move existing tasks to the list
- For existing task, open the task, then click on the "i" icon to access the options.
- Go down and click on **List** then choose from your new list.

Note: if you are not able to easily find a task, use the search bar option in the reminders app to find the task.

How to Add a List to a Group

Now you have created a list and moved the tasks to the list. However, there is more. You can add lists in same categories to a general group. So, for instance, you have a list containing anniversaries and another one containing birthdays, you can group both of them into an 'important date' group to keep your home page looking appealing.

Follow the easy steps below to create your group

- Go to the homepage for the **reminders app**

- At the right top corner of your screen, click on **Edit.**
- Then click on **Add Group** at the bottom left of your screen.
- Input your preferred group name and choose all the lists you want to add to the group.
- Then tap **Done.**
- To modify the lists in each group, click on **Edit** again.
- Then click on the "i" icon next to the group.
- Then remove or add lists using the *Include* option.

How to Use Swipe Typing

Another addition to the iOS 13 is the swipe typing feature in your device default keyboard. This feature allows you to type a word by swiping your fringe across the keys of your keyboard rather than tapping out each word. The keyboard world then sorts out the rest by deducing the right words you were trying and then inserting it into your message. Although it may take some time for you to get used to it, seeing that it is a new development, however once you get the hang of it, you would notice that it is actually faster than tapping each key.

Swipe typing is already enabled with the iOS 13 and so you would not need to take any action to turn it on. For instance, say you want to type "call", all you need to do is to tap on the "c" key with your keyboard the day your finger over the "a", "l" and "l" keys in this order. The keyboard world automatically predicts the words you wish to type.

One benefit of this feature is that is faster than tapping on different keys. The downside however is that swipe typing is not as accurate as the normal typing but there are available ways to take care of it. Once you are done swiping, the keyboard would present 3 options for the words you swiped and you click to choose the right one. If the prediction in the center is correct, continue to swipe your next words to select it automatically.

The longer you use the keyword the more accurate the predictions become, but when using uncommon words, you may likely have to tap type first. Although you can always alternate between swiping and swiping whenever you want to without changing any settings.

How to Disable Swipe Typing

While the swipe typing is enabled by default, you can disable it if you do not find it useful or easy.

- Go to the settings app.
- Click on **General.**
- Then select **Keyboards.**
- Navigate to **"Slide to Type"** and move the switch to the left to disable the option.

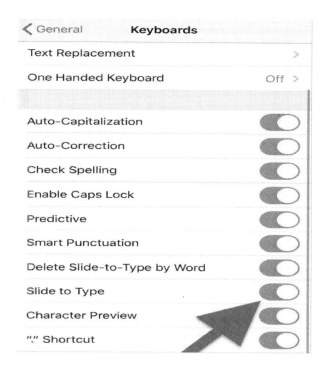

Another way to do this is by using the keyboard itself.

- Long press on the keyboard switcher.
- Then click on **Keyboard settings.**
- Depending on your keyboard setup, you would see the switcher as a Globe icon or an Emoji icon.
- Navigate to **"Slide to Type"** and move the switch to the left to disable the option.

Note: If you have only one keyboard activated on your device, you would be unable to use this option.

How to Remove Location Details from your Photos in iOS 13

When you take pictures with your iPad, the GPS records the exact place the photo was shot. This can be beneficial as you can view your photos based on location or occasion. It helps when sorting out photo shoots and also to help keep track of friends and family years after.

This also means that whenever you share these photos, viewers can find out where the photo was taken from their photo app. This may be an issue when posting photos to social media where most of your followers may be people you do not know personally and for security reasons you may not want to post a picture that can lead to your home.

The **iOS 13** has made it possible to remove location details from your photos or choose the persons you would like to have access to this information. You can remove location from your videos, photos, movies or multiple images that you intend to send via messages, Facebook, Mail, and so on with the steps below:

- Capture your photos in the normal way with your camera app.

- Go to the section where the photo was saved.

- If sharing a single video or photo, click on it to open, then click on the **Share** button.

- If sharing several videos and photos, click on **Select** in the section view, then click on all the items you wish to share and then click on the **Share** button.

- On the next screen to share, you would notice a new button for **Options.**

- Click on the **Options** and disable the **Location** on the next screen.

- Then select any media you like to send your photo through.

Note: You would have to set this feature each time you want to share a video or picture. The Location details can only be disabled from the iPad photo app so it is important that you always share your contents from the app directly. The photos and videos on your iPad would contain to have the location details as the feature only affects contents that you want to share to third party.

How to Set a Profile picture and Name in iMessages

With this feature, you can now set a screen name and a profile image on your iMessage that you would share with your selected contacts. So, when next you text another iPad user, they would not need to save your contact details before they can know who is texting them. Follow the easy steps below to set it up.

- Open the messages app.
- Click on the 3 dots (…) at the right upper corner of your screen.
- Then click on **Edit Name and Photo.**
- On the next screen, you can choose a profile picture and also input your desired last and first name.
- You can choose to use your personal Memoji as your profile picture or choose from available Animoji.
- Then, set if you would like to share this detail with any of the options on the screen: with *Anyone, Contacts Only,* or to *Always Ask* if the details is to be shared.

How to Create and Use Animoji or Memoji

The iPadOS/ iOS 13 has made it possible for every device that has the iOS 13 to be able to access the Animoji or Memoji as you do not need to have an iPad with TrueDepth selfie camera to be able to use this feature. So, you can now create a cartoon version of your loved ones or of self.

The steps below would show you how to create a Memoji

- go to name and profile picture settings.
- Click on the circle for pictures close to the name field.
- Then click on the "+" sign to make your own Memoji.

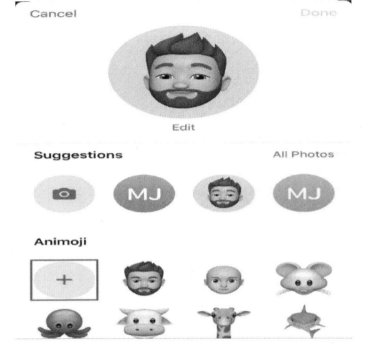

- After you must have created on, click on it to choose a pose for your Memoji and to also use it as your profile picture.

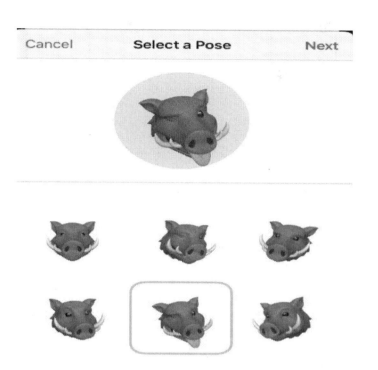

If you would rather use something else other than a picture of yourself, you can make use of the Animoji. In the Animoji menu selection, you would find several options to choose from including a shark, mouse and even a skull. Then pick a pose in a similar way with the Memoji.

After selecting an Animoji or Memoji, you have to scale it, place it to fit the circle then select a background color to finish the setup.

How to Set View for your Profile Picture and Name in iMessages

It is quite cool to have your profile picture and name set especially when messaging a friend, however you may not want an unknown person to have access to your real names or profile picture. Thankfully, there is a setting to limit who has access to what.

- Go to the settings for **Share Automatically,** then select from the 3 options available for sharing your name and profile picture.
- Go for **Contacts Only** if you would rather share this with only people in your contact list.
- The **Anyone** option means that everyone and anyone can access this information
- **Always Ask** would give you the option to personally choose people to share with. Each time you receive a message in your iPad and you open it, you would receive a small pop-up at the top of your screen asking if you would like to share your details with the sender. Click on **Share** to send your details across or click on "**X**" to refuse and shut down the message.

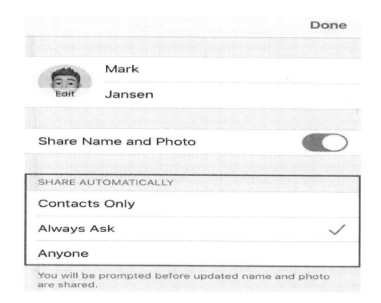

How to Download Fonts from the APP store

Fonts that you download from the app store are downloaded as apps. After downloading, you would see them in the formatting menu when using apps that support the downloaded fonts like Notes, emails etc. Follow the guide below to download fonts to your device.

- Go to the app store.
- Search for fonts by typing 'Fonts for iPad' in the search bar.
- Click on **GET** when you find a fonts app.

- For users that may have enabled Passcode, Face ID, or Touch ID on iTunes & App Store when installing apps, Apple would ask that you register for one of the 3 options before you can then install the fonts.
- After the Fonts app has been installed, click on **OPEN.**
- Give the required permissions to the app.
- Then click on the **'+' icon** at the left top side of your screen.
- Input a name for the collection then click on **OK.**
- On the next screen, click on the **'+' icon** at the left top side of your screen.
- You would see 2 options appear from the bottom: **Font Squirrel** and **Google Fonts.** Select **Google Fonts.**
- The next step is to choose the fonts you wish to add. While you can select multiple fonts, however, it is better to choose less than 10 fonts at a time. Once done, click on **'Add to collection.'**
- Then click on **OK.**

- Use the back arrow on your screen to Go back and then click on **'Install fonts'** at the bottom of your screen.
- This would take you to Safari browser where you would see a dialog box asking you to the configuration.
- Click on **'Allow.'**
- Once the download is completed, you would see a pop-up on your screen saying 'Profile Downloaded.'
- Click on **Close** to exit the app.
- Then go to the settings app on your iPad.
- Click on **General.**
- Then click on **Profile** towards the bottom of the next page.
- Click on the saved name for the downloaded fonts.
- Then click on **Install** at the right top corner of your screen.
- You may be prompted to input passcode, input the code and click on **Install** again.
- Once the installation is complete, click on **Done.**

- Return back to **Settings.**
- Click on **General.**
- Then select **Keyboard.**
- Click on **Keyboard** again on the next screen.
- Then click on **Add New Keyboard'**
- **Navigate to Fonts and click on it and your downloaded fonts are ready for use.**
- **Launch any messaging/ chat apps like the Message app.**
- **Click on your desired conversation or begin a new conversation.**
- **Long press on the Globe icon** at the left bottom corner of your screen, then chose **Fonts** from the list.
- You would see all available fonts above your keyboard.
- Select the font of your choice and begin to chat.

How to Enable Dark Mode

We wake up in the morning, eager to see our missed notifications, you pick your iPad and get almost blinded by the bright white theme of your iPad. Thankfully, the iOS 1e comes with a new dark mode that can save you from this brightness by changing the white areas in your iPad to a much darker tone. This change would apply to all the system apps including Safari and iMessages while Apple has encouraged all third-party developers to add themes that are compatible with the dark mode in their apps. Follow the steps below to find Dark Mode

- Go to the settings app
- Then click on **Display and Brightness**

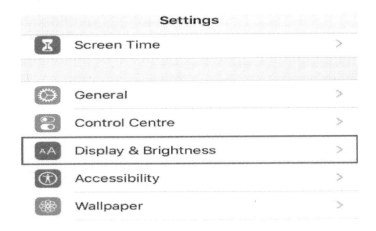

- Then tap on the tick box beneath the Light or Dark themes to activate your preferred option.

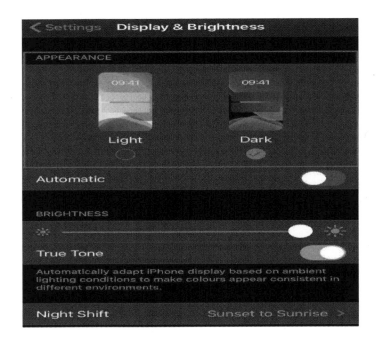

- If you want to set your iPad to have a bright theme in the day and a dark theme at night, just hit the toggle for the **Automatic** option and tap the **Options** button under **Automatic** to set when the darker theme should set in.
- Select either **Sunset to Sunrise** option or set to **Custom Schedule.**

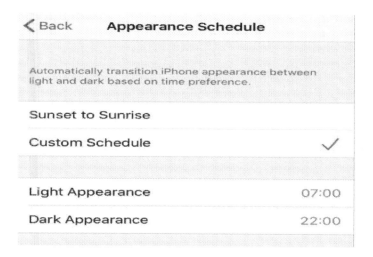

How to Automatically Activate the Dark Mode

If you wish to use a brighter theme during the day and a darker theme at night, you can do this without having to always go to settings every time to configure. You can configure your settings to interchange the two options at the set time. You can do this with the simple steps below:

- Go to the settings app
- Then click on **Display and Brightness**
- Beside the **Automatic** menu, move the switch to the right to enable it.
- The menu would by default change to **Sunset to Sunrise.**
- To edit this, click on **Options** under the **Automatic** menu.
- **Sunset to Sunrise** means that Dark Mode would be activated once the sun goes down using your GPS location.
- You can select *Custom Schedule* and input your own desired time for the Dark Mode to kick in.

How to Set Your Wallpaper to React to Dark Mode

Do you know that some wallpapers in the iOS 13 can react to the Dark Mode? Although small, it can be quite fun. To set a wallpaper that has a dynamic color changing feature, follow the simple steps below:

- Go to the settings app.

- Click on **Wallpapers.**

- Then select ***Choose a New Wallpaper.***

- *Then chose **Stills.***

- *Wallpapers that can react when the Dark Mode is enabled are marked with a bisected small circle at the right of your screen, towards the bottom and you would see a line down the image middle to display what changes you would get if activated.*

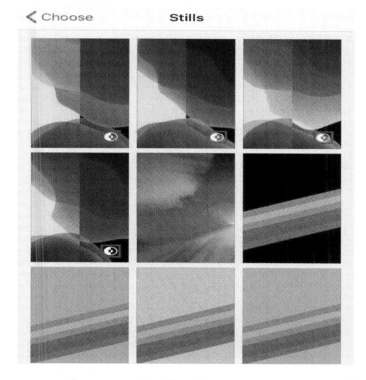

- If you would rather have your own customized wallpaper, return to the **Wallpaper menu**

- Navigate to *Dark Appearance Dims Wallpaper* and toggle the switch to the right to enable. Although the wallpapers would not react like the reacting ones, however, it would dim a little when the Dark mode is enabled so that you don't get dazzled by the lighter areas.

How to Set Optimized Battery Charging

With the iOS 13, you can optimize your battery charging to enable it last longer with the steps below:

- Launch the settings app.
- Click on **Battery.**
- Navigate to **Battery Health.**

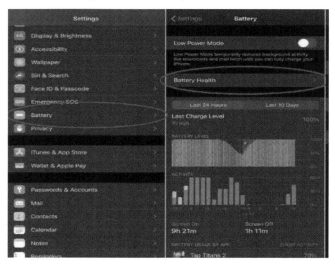

- Under **Battery Health,** you would find the maximum battery capacity left for your battery, an indication of the level of degradation as well as the option to enable Optimized Battery Charging.
- Move the switch beside **Optimized Battery Charging** to enable the feature.

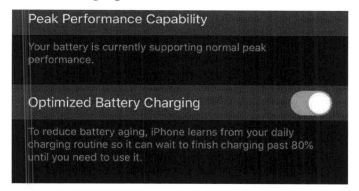

Note: while this feature is on, you may notice that your iPad could stop charging at 80%. You should not worry as Apple has ensured that the device does not drain battery quick.

Other Tips to Improve the Longevity of your iPad Battery

Several things work together to reduce the life of your battery like plugging the device even after it is fully charged. Below I would list tips that would help to prolong the life of the battery.

- It is important not to let your battery to totally get drained. Best is to always keep it at 0 percent and above.
- Avoid exposing the device to excessive heat. It is a very bad idea to charge your iPad in a very hot environment.
- Quick change from very hot to very cold condition is also very bad for the health of your battery.
- If you intend to not use your iPad for a week and above, it is advisable you run down the battery to below 80% but not less than 30 percent. Then shut down the iPad completely.
- Do not always fully charge your device when not using it for a long time.

How to Long Press App Icons to Reveal Menu Bar
Apple has activated the Peak feature and Haptic Touch across all the iPads. To get the contextual menu on your

iPad, simply click and hold on the iPad. To preview a link in Safari, click and hold on the link which would also show options to open the link in a new window, tap and more.

How to Pair your iPad with a DualShock 4

You can play games on your iPad using the DualShock 4 for a better experience. Follow the steps below to pair both devices.

- Go to the settings app.
- Click on **Bluetooth** to enable it.
- With the Bluetooth enabled, ensure that the DualShock 4 controller is well charged.
- Press both the share button and the PlayStation button at same time and hold down for some seconds.
- Then you would see the light at the back of the controller begin to flash intermittently.
- Under the Bluetooth menu on your iPad, you would see DualShock 4 Wireless controller come up as one of the devices.

- Click on it.
- The blinking light at the back of the controller should change to reddish pink color as an indicator that the devices are paired.

How to Disconnect a DualShock 4 from your iPad

After you are done with the game, it is advisable to turn off the Bluetooth connection. To disconnect through the controller, just hold down the PlayStation button for approximately 10 seconds.

To disconnect from your iPad, the best method would be to go through the Control Center with the steps below

- If using a Face ID compatible iPad, launch the control center by swiping diagonally from the top right to the lower left of your screen.
- If using a Touch ID compatible iPad, use your finger to swipe from the bottom up.
- Hold down the Bluetooth icon on your screen.
- A menu would pop up on your screen, hold down the icon for *Bluetooth: On.*

- Another pop up would show on the screen displaying **"DUALSHOCK 4 Wireless Controller"** in the list.
- Click on it to disconnect your controller.

Another method you can use is below

- Go to the settings app and click on **Bluetooth.**
- A pop up would appear on your screen, hold down the icon for *Bluetooth: On.*
- Another pop up would show on the screen displaying **"DUALSHOCK 4 Wireless Controller"** in the list.
- Click on it to disconnect your controller.

And again, another method can be found below

- Go to the settings app and click on **Bluetooth.**
- On the next screen, under the **My Devices** List, you would find "DUALSHOCK 4 Wireless Controller"
- At the right of this option, you would find an icon with "I" in a blue circle. Click on this icon.
- A menu would pop up, then select **Disconnect.**

When next you want to use the controller, simply press the PlayStation button to immediately connect.

How to Unpair the DualShock 4 from your iPad

Usually, the PlayStation may connect by accident when stuffed in your bag especially when on a trip. In such cases, it is advised to unpair first and then re-pair when you want to use it.

To unpair this device, follow the steps highlighted above to disconnect but rather then clicking on **Disconnect,** you should click on **"Forget This Device"**

How to Pair your iPad with an Xbox One S controller

- Go to the settings app.
- Click on **Bluetooth** to enable it.
- With the Bluetooth enabled, ensure that the **Xbox One controller** is well charged.
- Press the Xbox logo button to turn on the Xbox.
- You would see a wireless enrollment button located at the back of the controller. Press the button and hold it for some seconds.

- If the controller has been unpaired already from a different device, please skip this step as you can just press and hold the Xbox button to put it in pairing mode.
- Then you would see the light of the Xbox button begin to flash quickly.
- Under the Bluetooth menu on your iPad, you would see "Xbox Wireless Controller" come up as one of the devices.
- Click on it.
- Once it is paired correctly, the blinking light would stop and remain focused.

How to Disconnect Xbox One Controller from your iPad

After you are done with the game, it is advisable to turn off the Bluetooth connection. To disconnect through the controller, just hold down the Xbox button for approximately 10 seconds.

To disconnect from your iPad, the best method would be to go through the Control Center with the steps below

- If using a Face ID compatible iPad, launch the control center by swiping diagonally from the top right to the lower left of your screen.
- If using a Touch ID compatible iPad, use your finger to swipe from the bottom up.
- Hold down the Bluetooth icon on your screen.
- A menu would pop up on your screen, hold down the icon for *Bluetooth: On.*
- Another pop up would show on the screen displaying "Xbox Wireless Controller" in the list.
- Click on it to disconnect your controller.

And another method can be found below

- Go to the settings app and click on **Bluetooth.**
- On the next screen, under the **My Devices** List, you would find "Xbox Wireless Controller."
- At the right of this option, you would find an icon with "I" in a blue circle. Click on this icon.
- A menu would pop up, then select **Disconnect**.

To use this device again, simply press the Xbox button to get it working.

How to Unpair the Xbox Controller from your iPad

Usually, the controller may connect by accident when stuffed in your bag especially when on a trip. In such cases, it is advised to unpair first and then re-pair when you want to use it.

To unpair this device, follow the steps highlighted above to disconnect but rather then clicking on **Disconnect,** you should click on **"Forget This Device"**

How to Use the New Gestures for Copy, Cut, Paste, Redo and Undo

For most users, the iPad and iPhone has become the major way we communicate with people online as well as carry out other document features which is why it is important to have a good text management feature other than the "shake to undo" gesture in the old iOS.

With the iOS 13, Apple introduced the three-finger gesture to make it easy for typing. Once you get used to these features, you would enjoy communicating via your iPad.

How to Redo and Undo

The **shake to undo** gesture has not been removed from iOS, however the three-finger swipe gesture is sure to override it as users get used to this new addition.

- To undo, swipe to the left with your 3 fingers on the screen.
- To Redo, swipe to the right with your 3 fingers on the screen.
- Another way to undo is by double-clicking on the screen with your three fingers.
- If you look at the top of your screen, you would see the badges for "Redo" or "Undo" to verify your action.

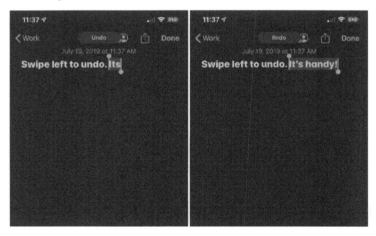

How to Copy, Cut and Paste

To best perform this feature, I would advise you use your two fingers and your thumb and this can be somewhat tricky if using a small screen.

- To copy, use your 3 fingers to pinch on the text and then un-pinch (expand) using your three fingers to Paste the copied text.

- Perform the copy gesture twice with your finger to cut out text. While the first gesture would copy the text, repeating it the second time would cut out the text.

- If you look at the top of your screen, you would see the badges for "Copy," "Cut," or "Paste" to verify your action.

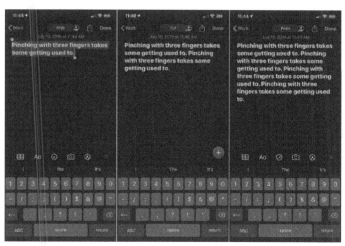

Cursor Movement on iPadOS/ iOS 13

The way the cursor is moved has also changed with the iOS 13. To drag around a text entry, simply click on the entry cursor. You no longer have to wait for some time before picking up text, once you touch it, you can move it immediately to where you want to place it.

Sadly, the little magnifying glass that pops up on the screen is no more and this can make it a little difficult to make a precise cursor placement as you would be unable to see the characters that you have picked.

How to Set the Compact Keyboard with Gesture Typing

Another addition to the iPadOS 13 is the new compact floating keyboard that you can reduce the size and also move around to your desired location. To get the keyboard in this mode, use your two fingers to pinch in on the keyboard. When you enter this mode, you can also make use of the gesture typing feature.

How to Access the Shortcut Bar

If you think that the gestures are difficult to use, then you can make use of the new shortcut bar. On any part of the screen, including the keyboard area, click and hold on the screen with your 3 fingers for approximately a second to launch the shortcut bar. The bar would appear above the screen with buttons for **Cut, Undo, Copy, Redo and Paste.** You will continue to see the bar as you repeat command and then disappears as soon as you enter text or move the cursor.

List of New Keyboard Shortcuts
During the WWDC conference, Apple noted that they included about 30 new shortcuts in Safari which has been compiled below for your reference.

- For the default font size in Reader (Cmd + 0)
- Increase Reader text size (Cmd + +)
- Decrease Reader text size (Cmd + -)
- Actual size (Cmd + 0)
- Toggle downloads (Cmd + Alt)
- Open link in background (Cmd + tap)
- Open link in new tab (Cmd + Shift + tap)
- Open link in new window (Cmd + Alt + tap)
- New Private tab (Cmd + Shift + N)
- Close other tabs (Cmd + Alt + W)
- Save webpage (Cmd + S)

- Zoom out (Cmd + -)
- Email this page (Cmd + I)
- Use selection for Find (Cmd + E)
- Zoom in (Cmd + +)
- Focus Smart Search field (Cmd + Alt + F)
- Close web view in app (Cmd + W)
- Change focused element (Alt + tab)
- To download linked file (Alt + tap)
- Add link to your Reading List (Shift + tap)
- Paste without formatting content (Cmd + Shift + Alt + V)
- To toggle bookmarks (Cmd + Alt + 1)
- Navigate around screen (arrow keys)
- Open search result (Cmd + Return)

How to Connect to Paired Bluetooth Devices from Control Center

It is now easier to access paired devices on iOS 13. As is usual, clicking on the Bluetooth button would either enable or disable Bluetooth. Now the iOS 13 has added the 3D Touch feature to display devices and also connect. With this new addition, you do not need to exit a current app to look for the settings app and all the long processes available in the other versions. Should you need to pair a device to Bluetooth, you can now do so from the control center without exiting the current app you are on. The steps are highlighted below:

- Launch the control center. If your iPad has a home button, just swipe from the bottom of your screen up to access the control center. If your iPad has no home button, swipe from the right top side of the iPad down to access control center.
- You either 3D touch or you click and hold the wireless connections block at the top right side of the screen to expand it.

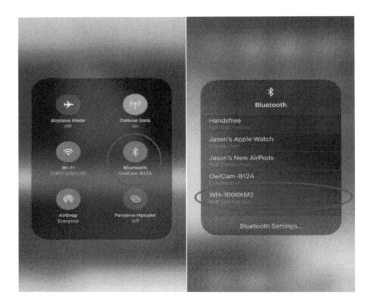

- 3D touch or Tap and hold the Bluetooth button at the right of the screen.
- You would see a list of all the Bluetooth devices that have been paired whether connected or not.
- Select the one you wish to connect to and you are fine.

How to Quickly Connect to Wi-Fi Through the Control Center

Most of us are used to joining new Wi-fi networks very frequently whether at a friend's place, a restaurant or while on a flight. The iOS 13 has now made it easier to connect. Rather than launching the settings app to be able to view the Wi-fi menu, you can now connect directly from the control center. Again, you would not need to exit an app to do this. See the steps below.

- Launch the control center. If your iPad has a home button, just swipe from the bottom of your screen up to access the control center. If your iPad has no home button, swipe from the right top side of the iPad down to access control center.
- You either 3D touch or you click and hold the wireless connections block at the top right side of the screen to expand it.
- 3D touch or Tap and hold the Wi-Fi button at the left side of your screen.

- You would see a list of all nearby Wi-fi networks that have been paired whether connected or not.
- Select the one you wish to connect to and you are fine.

How to Tap and Drag the New Volume Indicator

The new volume indicator introduced in the iOS 13 is less obtrusive and you can now pull it down and up. Several users have complained of the giant volume indicator for years now and Apple finally used a small vertical bar placed at the top left of the screen to replace it. Use your finger to drag the bar down and up. When you do this, an indicator would show at the end of the volume bar showing the output of your device sound, for example, Bluetooth device Airpods or speaker.

How to Download Large Apps over Cellular Network

You no longer have to wait for Wi-fi connection to be able to download large apps. Before now, your iOS would always warn you to connect to wi-fi to download large files but with the iOS 13, when downloading apps over 200MB, you would receive a pop up on your screen asking if you want to download with cellular or if you would rather wait for Wi-fi.

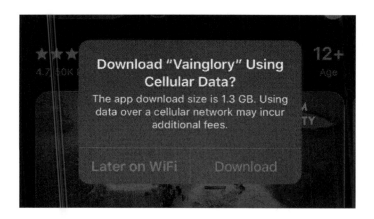

- Go to the settings app.
- Click on **iTunes & App Store.**

- Here, you can set the iOS to always allow you to download your apps over cellular or always ask you if you want to continue or ask you only when the app is over 200MB.

How to Scan Documents Straight to Files App

The new inbuilt scanner allows you to scan your documents, save as PDFs and even choose your preferred folder for storage. The upgraded to iOS 13 brought lots of improvement to the Files app but the one is being able to scan a document to PDF and being able to save it automatically in Files. To use this feature, follow the steps below.

- Go to the Files app.
- From any location in the app, pull down a little to display the options for view (View and Sorting style).
- Click on the 3-dot (…) icon at the left side of your screen, there, you would see the option to scan a document, create a new folder or connect to a server.

- Scan your receipts or forms as PDFs and get it saved in the cloud folder of your choice.

How to Unzip and Zip Files in the Files App

- Go to the files app.

- Click and hold down on a single file or select several files you want to compress.

- Then select **Compress** from the menu to create a zip file for all the files selected.

- Click on the **Share** button to share the zip file via email

- To unzip a file, click and hold down on the zipped file.

- Then click on **Uncompress** to unzip the file.

How to Organize Folders and Files in Local Storage

If you are like me that does a lot of work on my iPad, it means you would have several files and documents. This feature now makes it easy to organize folders and files in local storage. Before now, this option was only available for Dropbox or iCloud. Thankfully, you can create new folders on your local storage and be able to move the files around. To use this feature,

- Go to the files app.

- Go to the section for **On my iPad.**

- Then click and hold anywhere on your screen to display popup to create a new folder.

How to Markup with the Apple Pencil

Swipe from the bottom of the screen upwards to capture the screen.

How to Save Screenshots to the Files App

You can save all your screenshots in your Files app rather than the photos app. You can do this with the steps below:

- Take your screenshot then click on the little preview in the Markup to edit it.
- Then click on **Done.**
- You would see a new option on your screen, added to the **Delete Screenshot** and **Save to Photos** option, you would now have an option to **Save to Files.**
- The **Save to Files** option allows you to save the screenshots in your network folders or iCloud or other Files location outside the Photos app.

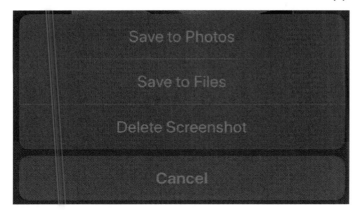

How to Zoom Voice Memos

If you use voice memos a lot, you may have always wanted to have more control over editing or trimming your voice memos. To do this,

- Go to your voice memo

- Click on edit and then you can pinch on the screen to zoom the waveform. This would give you better control and also make it easy for you to scrub through recordings that are very long.

When you launch the app store now, you would notice that the update section has been replaced with the Apple's Arcade gaming service. Follow the steps below to navigate to the updates section.

- Go to the App store app on your device.

- Click on your profile image at the top under the **Today section**.

- You would find the app updates at the bottom of the next screen.

- You can update all the apps if desired.

- To delete an app from your device, swipe left on the app to display the delete button

How to Delete Apps in iPadOS/ iOS 13

You can now delete apps from your device by

- long pressing on the desired app in your home screen to display an action to rearrange apps.
- Click on this option to get all the apps to wiggle while you would see an **X mark** beside each icon.
- Tap on the **X** beside the apps you wish to remove.

You can also delete apps from the App store. When viewing apps from the app store or updating apps, swipe to the left on any app you want to delete from the list to give you the option to **Delete.** This makes it convenient to delete any app you no longer need from your app store without having to exit the store. Let me explain the steps in details

- Go to the App store app on your device.

- Click on your account picture located at the right top corner of your screen.
- Navigate to the section for apps **Updated Recently.**
- To delete any app that was updated recently. Swipe to the left on the desire app in the list.
- Then click the red button that you see on your screen.

How to Delete Apps from the Update Screen

It is now more convenient to delete apps with the iOS 13. Although the usual way is still active but there is another way to save time.

- Go to the app store. You would see that the updates for app is now in your **Account card.** (click on your picture at the right top of your screen)
- If there are any apps on that list you want to delete, just pull the app to your left and an option would come up to delete the app.
- This applies to all the apps in the list whether it has a pending update or not.

How to Apply Filter to a Video

One of the additions in the iOS 13 is the filter tool. So now you can apply a filter similar to the ones used on Instagram in videos that you have captured already.

- Open the photo apps on your device.
- Choose a video from the photo library.
- Click on **Edit** at the right top side of your screen.

- Click on the Filter menu located at the end of your screen (it has a shape like a Venn diagram)

- Move through the available 9 filters to see how each would look on your video.

- Select your preferred filter and you would see a horizontal dial under the filter you selected.

- With your finger, slide the dial to adjust the level of intensity of that filter.

- Click on **Done** at the right bottom side of your screen to effect the filter on your video.

How to Use Lighting Mode Photo Effects

When you capture a picture while in portrait mode, the device makes use of the dual camera to create a depth-of-the-field effect which would allow you to create a photo that has a blurred background with a sharp subject. The iOS 13 introduced another feature called the High-Key Light Mono. This is a white and black effect like the Stage Light Mono but rather than add a black background, you would get a white background.

- Go to the Photo app on your device.

- Click on a portrait photo from your library to select it.

- Confirmed that the image was captured in a portrait mode by checking for the portrait label usually at the left top corner of your screen.

- Then click on **Edit** at the right top corner to go into an editing mode.

- Select the portrait icon in the tools at the bottom row then choose a lighting mode by sliding along the icons under the photos with your finger.
- After you have selected a lighting mode like the High-Key Light Mono effect, a slider would appear below it.
- Move your fingertip along the slider to rachet up or dial down the lighting effect intensity.
- Click on **Done** once you are satisfied with how the image looks.

Using the Block Feature in iPadOS/ iOS 13

How to Block Spam Calls

The new "silence unknown callers" feature is another addition to the iOS 13. With this feature, you can block spam calls without the need to block each one separately. This way, if you find out that the call is not actually spam, you can just go to your voicemails to check for the call and call back anyone that you need to contact. Follow the steps highlighted below to activate the new call blocker:

- Go to your settings app.
- Click on **Phone.**
- Then move the switch beside **Silence Unknown Callers** to the right to enable it.

Once this feature is active, unknown callers would be sent straight to voicemail by default and won't have to worry about robocalls, spam calls and other distractions would no longer bother you.

How to Block Spam, Contacts and Unknown Senders in Mail App

This feature would set the incoming emails from the blocked senders to go directly to the thrash folder. You are not really blocking the senders as you can always view the messages in the thrash folder. This option is better than totally blocking the contact. Currently, Apple has grouped all spammers and contacts that are blocked into a single folder. So, if in the past you blocked some phone numbers in Messages, FaceTime or Phone, you would see them along with the blocked senders for mails.

The first step is to select your block settings. This has to do with setting what you want the mail app to do with the blocked contacts.

- Go to the settings app.
- Click on **Mail.**

- Then navigate to **Threading.**
- Click on **Blocked Sender** and you would see 3 options

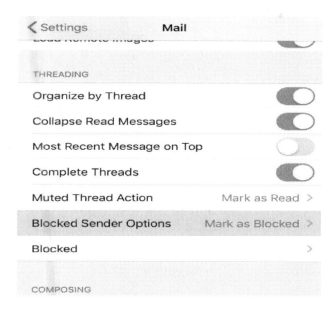

- If you choose **None,** it would disable email blocking.
- **"Mark as Blocked, Leave in Inbox"** means that the emails would come to your inbox but you would not be notified like the other emails.
- **Move to Trash,** would move emails from blocked contacts to your thrash folder. You can then set to manually empty the folder or have it deleted automatically.

Note: this feature would apply to all the accounts you have in your mail app including Outlook, Gmail, Yahoo etc.

How to Block a Sender Through Received Emails
When you receive an email from someone you do not know or do not want to hear from again, you can block the person from the email.

- Click on the contact fields at the top of the email to show you all the parties in the send list.
- Then click on the email address you want to block.
- The next screen would show you an expanded menu option.
- Click on **Block this contact.**
- Click on it again in the prompt to confirm your action.
- The contact is blocked!
- All emails from the sender whether present or past would have a blocked hand icon close to the date in the header for email. You would also see a notification at the top of the email reading, **"This message is from a sender in your blocked list."**

How to Unblock a Sender Through Received Email

If you change your mind about a sender, simply go back to the sender's contact details in the email and click on "Unblock this Contact." It may take some seconds for the hand icon to disappear but the sender would be unblocked instantly.

How to Block a Contact from Email Settings

In a case you do not have any email from the person you want to block, you can go to settings to stop them from sending any more messages.

- From the settings app, click on **Mail.**
- Then scroll down and click on **Blocked.**
- You would see all the email addresses and phone numbers that you have ever blocked in this screen.
- At the bottom of your screen, click on **"Add New."**
- Then select the contacts you want to block once prompted.

- You would then see the numbers and email addresses in the blocked list.

Note: if you do not have the contact of the person saved on your iPad, you would need to follow the first option to block them directly from inbox. This option only works with saved contacts.

How to Unblock a Contact from Settings

You can unblock all categories of blocked people from your settings since every single contacts or senders blocked get to share on the settings menu. To do this, follow the steps above to access the list of your blocked contacts.

- The short-swipe from the left on the email address or phone number you want to want to unblock.
- Then click on **Unblock.**
- Another way is to long swipe on the contact to automatically unblock it.
- Or you can click on **Edit** at the right top of your screen, click on the red "-" minus button beside

the email address or phone number you want to
unblock, then click on **Unblock.**

How to Use Better Formatting Features in Mail App

The mail app on the iPad now offers same formatting
options available in Mac

- Go to the compose box.

- Click on the **"Aa"** icon on the toolbar to show all
  the available formatting options

- You can now change the font size, font,
  indentation, color, formatting and others.

Operating the Safari Browser in iPadOS/ iOS 13

How to Auto Close Open Tabs in Safari

Launch the Safari browser on your iPad and click on the
View Tabs. If you are like me, you probably have several
open tabs from search results to opened social media
posts and so on. Some you want to close but could be
quite tiring to close each individually. Thankfully, iOS

added a feature to automatically close open tabs in the Safari after a defined time. Follow the steps to activate

- Go to the settings app.

- Navigate to Safari setting and click on it.

- You would see several options, navigate to the **Tabs** option, then click on **Close Tabs.**

- On the next screen, you would find further options, by default the selection is set to **Manually.**

- You can set to your preferred either **After One Week, After One Day or After One Month.**

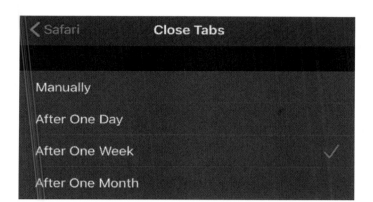

- There is no right or wrong selection. All depends on your usage, for me, I know that most times I never get to go back to the tabs after a week which is why I selected the **After one week** option.

How to Change the Default Location for Downloads from Safari

by default, every download from Safari goes to the **Download folder** in the iCloud drive, but you can modify the location to your preference even if you want it saved in your iPad's local storage. To do this,

- Go to settings.
- Click on **Safari.**

- Go to the **General** option and you would see option for **Downloads.**
- Here, you can choose the folders you want the downloaded files to go to.

How to Access Website Settings for Safari

the iPadOS 13 launch brought some additional features to the Safari browser. One of such change is being able to customize settings for individual sites. Similar to what we have on Safari on Mac, you can now modify different security and viewing options for different websites from the website settings. Safari would them automatically apply the settings so that you do not have to repeat them. I have highlighted the steps below

- Go to a site that you visit regularly.
- Click on the "aA" icon at the left top corner of your screen to show the **View menu** of the website.
- Then click on **Website settings.**

- **Reader Mode** option helps to make online articles more readable by removing extraneous web page contents from it. You can enable this icon by clicking on **"Use Reader Automatically"** to activate this feature by default.

- **Request Desktop Website:** click on this to view original desktop versions of a website on your mobile device.

- **Camera, Microphone, Location:** these last 3 options allows you to choose if you want sites to have access to your device microphone, camera as well as if the sites should be able to know your location. You can choose either **Deny** or **Allow,** but if you would rather change your options per

153

time, then you should select the option for **Ask.**
This way, whenever sites want to access these
features, Safari would first seek your consent.

How to Access Safari Download Manager

Those who use the Safari desktop version would be
more familiar with the Downloads pane in the browser,
which informs you on items that have been downloaded
and that are currently downloading. Now you can see
such with the mobile version of the browser. When you
want to download a file, you would see a little download
icon at the right top corner of your screen.

Click on the icon to see the status of your downloads,
click on the magnifying glass close to the downloaded
file to go to the folder where the download is located
either on the cloud or on your iPad.

How to Download Files Using Safari

Another great addition to the iPadOS and iOS 13 is the
new download manager available in Safari.

- Whenever you open any downloadable link, you
  would get a popup on your screen asking if you
  want the file downloaded.

- Then click on **Download** to begin downloading the file.

- You would see a **Download** icon in your toolbar while the file is downloading.

- Click on the download icon to show the progress of the Downloads.

- Go to the **Downloads** folder of your Files app to access the downloaded contents.

- All downloaded items from Safari are stored on the device local storage.

How to Modify when the Downloaded File List in Safari is Cleared

The upgrade introduced a Download manager in the mobile version of the Safari browser similar to what is obtainable in Windows and Mac. By default, the list is cleared at the end of each day, however, you can set it to clear the list once the download is done or go for the manual way of clearing lists.

- Go to the settings app.

- Click on **Safari.**

- Then click on **Downloads.**

- Click on **Remove Download List Items**.

- Select any of the options on your screen, Upon
  successful download, After one day, or Manually.

By default, all downloaded files are saved in the **Download folder** of the Files app but you can modify this by selecting an alternative storage location in the settings screen.

How to Modify Where Downloaded Files from Safari are Saved

By default, all downloaded files are saved in the **Download folder** of the Files app but you can modify this by selecting an alternative storage location with the steps below:

- Go to the settings app.
- Click on **Safari.**
- Then click on **Downloads.**

- You can then make your choice from the available options: **On My iPad,** iCloud Drive, or in another location that you want.

How to Disable Content Blockers Temporarily in Safari

Content blockers are used to stop ads like banners and popups from loading on any website you visit. It may also disable beacons, cookies and other to protect your privacy and prevent the site from tracking you online. Sometimes, the feature may block an element that you need to access like a web form. If you notice that a useful page element is not coming up because of the content blocker, you can disable it temporarily with the steps below:

- Go to the Safari browser and type in the desired site to visit
- Click on the "aA" icon at the left top corner of your screen to show the View menu of that site.
- Click on" **Turn Off Content Blockers."**

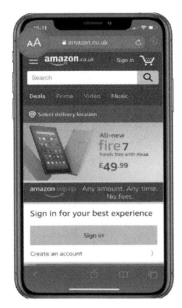

- If you want this disabled for a particular website only, click on **Website Settings** and then move the switch beside **Use Content Blockers** to the left to disable it.

How to Enable Content Blockers in Safari

- Go to the settings app.
- Click on **Safari.**

- Go to the **General** option and click on **Content Blockers.**

- Move the switch beside it to the right to enable the option

Note: this option would not be available if you do not install a minimum of one 3rd party content blocker from the store.

How to Share or Save a Safari Web Page as a PDF

this option is only available with the Safari browser and does not include other third-party browsers. Follow the steps to access this feature.

- Open the Safari app on your device.
- Go to the webpage you want to save as PDF.
- Press both the Sleep/wake button and the Home button at same time to take a screenshot.
- If your device does not have a home button, use both the volume up and the power button to take your screenshot.
- You would see a preview of the screenshot at the left lower side of the screen.
- Click on the preview to launch the **Instant Markup Interface,** you have only 5 secs before this screen disappears.
- Click on the **Full-Page** option in the right upper corner of the Markup interface.
- Click on **Done** and then select **Save PDF to Files** to save as PDF.

- Click on the **Share** button to share the PDF and choose who and how you want to share it from that screen.

Conclusion

Now that you are more familiar with features and tips on operating your iPad Pro, I am confident that you would enjoy operating your device.

All relevant areas concerning the new iPadOS and iOS 13 on your iPad Pro has been carefully outlined and discussed in details to make users more familiar with its operations as well as other information not contained elsewhere.

If you are pleased with the content of this book, don't forget to recommend this book to a friend.

Thank you.

Other Books by the Same Author

- iPhone 11 User Guide https://amzn.to/2mBZOME
- iPhone 11 Pro Max User Guide
  https://amzn.to/2lSEBOc
- iOS 13 User Guide https://amzn.to/2nxY9Yw
- Apple TV 4K/ HD User Guide
  https://amzn.to/2kqpBq4
- Amazon Echo Dot 3rd Generation User Guide
  https://amzn.to/2kE3X1T
- Kindle Oasis 3 10th Generation User Guide
  https://amzn.to/2kGM42w
- Mastering your iPhone XR for beginners, seniors
  and new iPhone users https://amzn.to/2mgegtc
- Samsung Note 10 and Note 10 Plus User Guide
  https://amzn.to/2mjBTRG
- Fire TV Stick User Guide
  https://amzn.to/2kQwTDP

Printed in Great
Britain
by Amazon

32468731R00099